the

Beginner's Guide
to Google Ads

by Discosloth co-founder

ANYA GILDNER

ISBN 978-1-7337948-0-0

Published by Baltika Press
www.baltikapress.com

Printed in the United States of America.

CONTENTS

Introduction

So you want to learn search marketing!

Let's be honest - I didn't grow up wanting to be a search engine marketer when I was older, but that's mostly because it didn't even exist at the time. I did love computers, though, and as I entered the world of digital marketing I became fascinated with the concept of pay-per-click advertising.

It was a slow start for me: of course, in college one doesn't learn anything about advanced digital concepts, so in order to be successful you also need to be driven, self-starting, ambitious, and know where to go to learn everything you need to know about different ad channels and bidding strategies and analytics and everything else.

In 2017, my husband and I cofounded a search marketing company called Discosloth. We had both been working in marketing for years, and we were getting tired of working for the man. We knew we could do better work on our own, where we could call the shots and employ the strategies we knew worked best.

Two years later, and our small agency has grown exponentially. We are still a small team (with three full-timers and a handful of freelancers) but we have worked with companies on every continent (except Antarctica!) and manage several millions in ad spend. We've built a lovely framework for Discosloth, where every employee can work remotely and enjoy going to work from the comfort of their sofa in Austin, a beach in Mexico or Greece, an Airbnb in St Petersburg, or wherever else we happen to want to be.

And that's the beauty of digital marketing - learning how to make sales from afar is one of the craziest things about the internet. You, too, can learn PPC. Whether you own your own online ecommerce store, whether you're an entry-level marketer, or whether you're a small business owner trying to get a handle on internet sales, learning Google Ads or Microsoft Ads is a powerful tool in your marketing arsenal.

In 2018, Gil and I wrote the Beginner's Guide To PPC, an online guide that was released for totally free. The feedback was crazy - we had thousands of readers almost overnight. As an agency, we have a strong content marketing strategy, and this was one of our most successful launches. It garnered some rave reviews. Rand Fishkin said "this was the one" for those needing to learn PPC. Steven Kenwright said "this was the sort of content I wish I'd created". Both extremely high praise that we were beyond excited to receive. I think that the guide received such great feedback because there was a huge hole in the educational material available for learning PPC marketing. See, when we were researching what was available out there, we could only find $300 courses (the types done by marketing gurus) or blog posts of questionable reliability. There wasn't a single definitive, detailed guide that covered everything you really needed to know.

In this book, we've added extensive information about the ever-changing aspects of Google Ads and Microsoft Ads. Everything changes - since we published that online guide, even the names have changed from Google AdWords and Bing Ads to Google Ads and Microsoft Ads.

Additionally, we've heard a lot of people voicing concern about automation, and the role it will play in both PPC itself, and the PPC specialists who themselves have to work with it on a daily basis. Our automation chapter addresses the pros and cons of automation as need in Google Ads, specifically.

I've also added a bit about privacy, because it's a growing concern and something I'm personally very interested in. We'll look at how closely you can actually target, and whether such hyper-focused targeting is actually even necessary or beneficial for the vast majority of advertising campaigns.

Whether you're a small business owner, a marketing professional brushing up on digital techniques, or a student, this guide will serve as a comprehensive resource for understanding the strategy behind profitable Google Ads campaigns...all of which can then be applied further to other PPC platforms like Microsoft Ads, Yandex.Direct, or even LinkedIn or Twitter ads.

This guide goes through the entire advertising process, from initial keyword research to analyzing data from results. We place an emphasis on strategy - the why - over the how. We'll use an imaginary client - Anya's Organic Juices - which will establish best practices for a simple ecommerce campaign and let us learn more about keyword research, campaign structure, ad writing, and different campaign types among other things.

That said, let's jump into it and start learning how to build a campaign!

Chapter 1: What To Know Before You Start Google Ads

1.1 How does this guide work?

We will spend the first two chapters going over strategy. Beginning in Chapter 3, we'll dig into the actual nuts and bolts of putting a campaign together.

We're going to go through the entire campaign process, from keyword research to performance analysis, using an imaginary client Anya's Organics.

Anya's Organics is a small Californian juice company that bottles their own juice. They currently sell in stores, but they recently built an ecommerce website to start expanding across the entire West Coast (where all the hippies are). We'll help Anya's Organics implement their campaign, and by following along you'll learn how to do just the same!

The Beginner's Guide To Google Ads will teach you all of the basic thought processes required to set up an efficient, optimizable, and profitable pay-per-click campaign.

This guide isn't about which buttons to click and interface panels to open. It's not going to tell you specific processes like how to filter data by campaign name, for example. You can just Google things like that.

It's like playing baseball. Anyone can pick up a bat and learn how to hit a ball. But how do you win a game? Just having technical skill gets you nowhere. Strategy and psychology is the crucial element behind a winning team.

In this guide, we're going to talk more about the strategy and psychology behind a profitable PPC campaign. If you're just searching for setup instructions, there are plenty of them created directly by Google, which we link to in our resource chapter.

PPC (pay-per-click) is a tool that helps you get in front of your customers. You can use it to promote your business, sell your services, increase brand awareness or just get more traffic to your website or app...or even your offline grocery store.

1.2 What is PPC and how does it work?

PPC advertising is the way in which companies display their ads in search engines and other platforms. The most effective ads show when a user is searching for their products or services, or for other closely related search queries.

PPC stands for "pay per click". It means that the advertiser pays only when someone clicks directly on the ad. It's an easy way of getting users to your website, without waiting for your website to be visible organically.

The most known PPC "providers" are search networks, like Google, Bing, Baidu, Yandex, Facebook, or Instagram. In a nutshell, advertisers bid in an auction for ad placement. Your position in the searches is based on your bid (how much you're willing to pay for a click) and on your ads & website's relevancy (aka Quality Score).

Google and the other leading search engines have an automated algorithm that is basically an invisible auction. The higher your bid, the higher position in the searches you get. The only difference is that Google is also attributing a Quality Score to all of your keywords. So the final formula that calculates your position (Ad Rank) is: *Bid x Quality Score = Rank.*

The benefit is that even with a lower bid, as long as you have good ads and a website that's highly targeted to your audience, you can get a better position than someone with higher bids.

The Quality Score is an estimation of the quality of your ads, keywords and landing page on a scale of 1-10. It will look at expected clickthrough rate, ad relevance, and landing page experience to determine your score.

1.3 Can I do Google Ads for my own business?

Of course! But it doesn't matter if you've decided to do it yourself, or hire an agency or a freelancer. If you're spending money on PPC, you need to know how paid advertising works and how your campaign should look like. This course should guide you through the process of creating a campaign from scratch, but most of all it will help you understand the logic behind it. Setting up campaigns is not just clicking different buttons and adding the first keywords that come to your mind and seem relevant. It's about research and understanding your customer's struggles and needs.

At the end of this course, you'll find a full list of useful resources for you to use! Have fun with it.

It's important to understand that PPC (as with any other type of marketing) cannot be learned by reading a book or watching tutorials. It's a very hands-on process. Tutorials will help you avoid making some major mistakes, but hopefully this guide will give you enough knowledge so that when you start working with something like Google Ads you can just as easily "figure it out by yourself" without wasting too much money.

That's why we've decided to show how to create a real campaign, and explain every part of its creation, from keyword research to campaign setup to analyzing the actual results.

1.4 Does my website need Google Ads?

To be clear, the fact that you've created an account and created a good campaign doesn't guarantee you will get sales. There are lots of things to consider and think about before you decide to invest in it. Do you have an existing brand? If no one has ever heard of you, they might not want to spend their money on your website. The internet is full of scammers and low quality products. How can you stand out from them? There are a few common reasons why even the best PPC campaign won't work for you:

• Your website has bad grammar/empty sections/low

quality images/low quality content/buttons not working, etc.

- If someone searches for your brand they see bad reviews about you on other websites.
- Your website is hard to navigate. There are too many options online for users to spend time figuring out how to use your website.
- Low page loading speed. You can evaluate your page speed with Google's PageSpeed Insights. Also, Pingdom will give you very good insights on what is broken.
- Your website is not optimized for mobile. You can use Google's Mobile-Friendly Test to check this. Also make sure you check your mobile speed too.

Some people forget how important is for websites to be optimized for mobile. Based on Statista research, in 2018, 52.2 percent of website traffic worldwide was generated through mobile phones, up from 50.3 percent in the previous year. You know what I'm saying?

1.5 I'm doing SEO, do I still need to spend on paid?

To get the best conversion rates and increase your brand trust, you need visibility on all channels that make sense to your business model.

If you have good paid campaigns and no SEO, users might not trust you, as your online presence is limited to ads. If you do SEO and no paid advertising, it might take you forever (possibly years) to get in front of your clients.

The first thing that's important to keep in mind: users won't necessarily see you online once, and buy right away. Just use your own browsing habits as a reference. Do you ever click on an ad and make a purchase without any further research? For a brand you've never heard about? The answer is most probably NO!

We'll talk about this in a later chapter, but it's important to understand the idea of multi-channel attribution. In short, it helps you see all the channels that users use before they convert on your website.

Someone's journey might look like this:

For some it's more like:

Beyond giving you visibility on multiple channels, SEO helps you create a brand and be useful, informative and educational. Let's look at two scenarios.

Let's say someone came to your website via an ad. They've never heard of you before. All you have on the website is a landing page with a big button saying "Buy Now" and some bullet points saying how awesome you are.

The second scenario: someone came to your website via an ad. They've also never heard of you before. They get to your website and can see the product they've searched for. They see an entire page describing benefits in detail, maybe even a link to some studies proving what you say. You also have a blog section where you explain how to use it, or who it won't work for. And then they Google your brand, and they can see other people writing about their experience of buying the same product from you. This is all a part of SEO!

Can you see how that can increase your conversion rate? And also, why a good paid campaign is not always enough to get good results?

The third thing to consider is how paid advertising can help your SEO efforts. Paid advertising can help you quickly test specific keywords, phrases, audiences or even business ideas. Once you see which one works, you can do more SEO around it, creating content and so on while already knowing that there is demand for the idea.

Chapter 2: How People See Advertising

2.1 Why did we learn to ignore ads?

If you've spent any amount of time in the digital marketing world, you've probably heard about terms like "banner blindness" or "advertising blindness". But what does it actually mean, and how can we fight it?

I have to confess that I create online ads for a living, and I also use an ad blocker. Who wouldn't? One of the benefits of using an ad blocker is that you can see the exact amount of ads that have been blocked on each page.

Guess how many ads you see while watching a YouTube video? Maybe five or ten? No, right now Opera is telling me it's blocked 55 ads on just ONE video. We see thousands of ads per day. Long ago we started, consciously or not, trying to ignore web advertising.

Ad blindness is the phenomenon of users ignoring every ad they see, or anything that even looks like an ad. Ad blindness on the internet developed along with the rise of ads themselves. The more you see, the more you ignore. It doesn't mean that, as advertisers, we don't have a chance.

We still have the possibility of gaining visibility. We

just need to understand that as the internet evolves, customers evolve too and are smarter about how it works. So should our ads. No one likes being told what to do! And we most certainly don't want to see 55 different companies telling us what to do.

The first thing to remember is that salesy ads don't work anymore.

Users want to be educated, entertained, and informed. Or, they just want to feel something (happiness, sadness, nostalgia, etc). Whether it's a video, display ad, or even just a search ad, today's audiences want to be given a chance to choose the product by its benefits, and not just which ad can write BUY NOW or CLICK HERE with a bigger font.

Now, we'll go over some of the most common ad formats that we can use in Google Ads.

2.2 What are search ads?

Search advertising ads are placed within a search engine's results page. They have a similar format as organic results (unpaid) and are usually on the top (first 3-4 results) and sometimes a few on the bottom of the results.

Anya's Organic Kombucha | 10% Off On All Repeat Orders
Ad www.anyasorganic.com/kombucha
The Only 100% Organic, 100% Cold Pressed and 100% Californian. Order Now Online!
No Additives · 100% Organic Juice · No Artificial Sugars · No Preservatives

How We Do It
Our fresh fruit is sourced directly from 100% organic growers.

Benefits
Learn more about why organic is good for you and our environment

Gift Card
Give a healthy 100% Californian and Organic gift to a friend.

Wholesale
Your customers will love our delicious, healthy juices & drinks.

Search ads work based on the search term entered into

the search engine. The most popular search engines are Google, Bing, Yandex, Baidu, Yahoo, and DuckDuckGo.

The benefit of search ads is that you can respond directly to someone's issues, questions or needs. As opposed to social media advertising, you don't have to convince your audience that they need detox juices: they already know that, and are looking for some to buy.

2.3 What are display ads?

Display ads (or display advertising) is a form of online advertising on websites or apps that use image ads, rich media ads, video ads or text ads. Google's display advertising reach 80% of global internet users.

Display ads catch users whenever they are surfing online, but not searching for a specific product or service. Because of this the main goal of display advertising should not be getting clicks, but to drive brand awareness.

There are multiple ways you can target users via display advertising. One of the most important is remarketing. Remarketing is used for websites that want to remind previous users about themselves. It can be used to target users that visited a specific product on your website but didn't purchase, and "follow them" around the internet showing the exact product they were interested in.

You can target users based on:
- their interests and habits
- what they're actively researching
- how they've interacted with your business

We won't cover display ad formats in detail as they change constantly, but you can see more formats on Google's site.

2.4 What are shopping ads?

Shopping ads are a type of ads that show more detailed information about the product you sell. Usually Shopping ads contain an image, price, brand, a title and links directly to the item in your store. The ads are shown on top of the search engines. It's not available in all countries, so check the availability before you start. Most shopping ads are created on Google, although Bing has an option for it too.

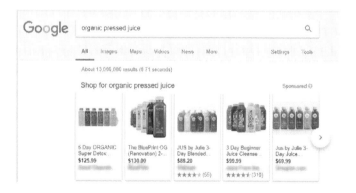

Before you start, you'll need to create a Merchant Center account where you'll upload all details about the products you want to advertise. Make sure you follow the guidelines or your product will be rejected.

These type of ads work very well, as they give your audience a visual aspect of the product before clicking. The downside is that you cannot target specific keywords. Google will choose what search queries you ads will appear for based on the product description and title.

2.5 What are video ads?

Video ads (or video advertising) are mostly known as YouTube ads. They appear when someone is searching or watching a YouTube video. Instead of per click, you pay for each view. The ads are created via Google Ads.

Same as display ads, the benefit of running YouTube ads is not in getting clicks or sales. It's about brand awareness...and possibly annoying people that just want to listen to some music.

It's very important to execute video ads correctly, as users ignore most ads on YouTube. You want to make sure you create something that will catch their attention in the first 2 seconds. The approach is different than TV ads. Since they're skippable (unlike TV ads) they need to be catchy, funny, smart, and speak to a user's emotions more than anything else. A common fault of YouTube advertisers is going into too much detail or making a video too long.

Our imaginary client, Anya's Organics, was thinking about a YouTube campaign. They already had a 30-second TV spot produced, but this video wouldn't do well on YouTube. Anya's Organics needs a short, 15-second, inspirational ad with a primary focus on branding rather than sales. Views are extremely cheap and highly targetable on YouTube, which means someone who sees an Anya's Organics video will also likely see some search ads later on, as well!

You can also target users that have already visited your website (remarketing), based on specific interests, or even just a specific channel.

Chapter 3: Keyword Research & Analysis For PPC

3.1 How the way we search changed

One of the most important parts of any online marketing campaign is keyword research. If you know who your audience is & how they search for your service, 80% of your work is done.

Together with Google's continual algorithm updates and the technology used to interpret our search results, the way we actually use search has drastically changed.

If in 2006 we used keywords to search for information (like typing in "organic juice"), now we ask questions and actually talk to the search engine. Our searches now look more like "where can I buy organic juice?"

As it changes, the way to create campaigns and the way we do our research changes too. We don't just target our product's name, but we target people's questions about what we can offer. This will only continue to be important as voice search becomes more common.

The research helps you create useful content for your user, but it also helps you choose the right keywords you need to target for your paid campaigns.

If you're a lawyer with a focus on gender discrimination, you'd probably think about targeting "gender discrimination lawyer", but what you should actually target are specific searches like: "i got fired for being pregnant".

3.2 *Where to start with research*

We'll use Anya's Organics campaign as an example. So, we're a creating a campaign for a website that sells different types of organic juices.

Since Anya's Organic is a small company just now entering the world of PPC, our initial budget is $1,500 per month, targeting the United States. The juices on the website are separated into a few categories: Cleanse Packs, Cold Pressed Juices, Organic Soft Drinks and Organic Kombucha.

Before we start researching the keywords, we want to have a better understanding of our audience. Who are buying these products? What else are they interested in? Where do we find these people hanging out? And very importantly, what is the reason behind them buying this product?

Before you start, create a document with your main products (category) and a column for all negative keywords you can find. Ours would look like this:

Cleanse Packs	Cold Pressed Juices	Organic Soft Drinks	Organic Kombucha	Negatives

The list will be updated and changed during the research process.

3.3 Tools & techniques

Google Keyword Planner

The first tool everyone uses in making a Google Ads campaign is the Google Keyword Planner. It's totally free. Just make sure you use it in an active account with payment details already set up, otherwise the suggestions you'll get will be very broad. You can find the tool in your Google Ads account.

The Keyword Planner is a very good way to start your research. It helps get ideas on how users search and gives you some phrasing variations that you might not have thought about. It also can be a good resource for negative keywords. Let's start with researching how people are searching for "Cold Pressed Juices".

In the example, we find that some users search for "cold press juicer". As we are selling juices, not machines, we don't want to appear for anyone searching for "juicers" so it goes to our Negative Keywords column.

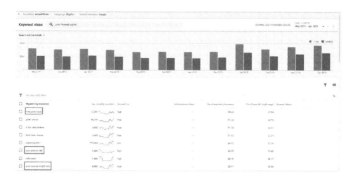

"Juice cleanse diet" and "juice cleanse weight loss" are good keywords, but users might be more interested in information rather than buying a specific product. So the conversion rate will be lower for those searches. If we have a bigger budget, we might want to create a separate ad group for those so we can track the performance separately and limit the budget for it. But for now, we'll wait since those searches seem like they're from people looking for education rather than purchasing.

We also notice that users are searching for "3 day juice cleanse", Make sure you have a specific product for this, and add these keywords to the Juice Cleanse ad group.

From just one search, we've added this to our list:

Cleanse Packs	Juice Cleanse Diet (maybe)	Cold Pressed Juices	Organic Soft Drinks	Organic Kombucha	Negatives
3 day juice cleanse	juice cleanse diet				juicer
juice cleanse	juice cleanse weight loss				
best juice cleanse					

Once you've got your ideas in the Keywords Planner, Google them!

The first thing to use is Google Auto Suggest. It's a great place to search for inspiration and to see what people are searching for. If you're searching for ideas, use an asterisk to get ideas for unknown or variable words:

Or just use a letter:

Add every letter from the alphabet at the end of the keywords you are researching:

Now, we have even more info to add to our sheet. We know that we don't want to appear for "avenue", "vape", "recipes", "whole foods" and all the locations that we are not targeting. But we've learnt some other common words that these organic hippies use. Like "organic fruit juice", "juice cleanse delivery" and more.

By the end of this exercise you'll have an amazing list of negatives (this is very, very important) and different variations on how users search.

The second way to use Google is by using the infinite "People Also Ask" boxes for even more ideas.

Even if you cannot use all the suggestions as your keywords, make sure your website answers the main questions users ask. It will help with both your organic traffic and user trust and retention. Once someone clicks on your ad, based on what info they find on your website they'll decide if they can trust you or not.

Microsoft Ads Keyword Planner

Bing (or Microsoft Ads) is a thing! And it can give you some additional insights on what you're searching for. Bing works very similarly to Google Ads Keyword Planner, you can find it in Bing's (or Microsoft now…it's easy to lose track) tools section. Choose your targeting area and the keyword and you'll see suggestions on both volume and bid levels for the keyword.

Answer the Public

Answer the Public (which is freely available at answerthepublic.com) is a very useful website, and we really like the design (maybe this part isn't helpful for your research...but we still like it a lot). As they say on the homepage, "Enter your keyword & he'll suggest content ideas in seconds." You'll get something like this:

Research your existing audience

If you already have existing traffic, we start with

Google Analytics data. For those not in the know, Google Analytics (or GA) is a plugin used by millions of websites to track user activity and engagement.

If you go to the Audience tab, you can learn more about your demographics. For example, for Anya's Organic Juices we can see that our main audience are women aged 25-34:

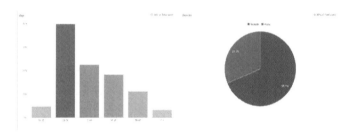

You might have noticed that we see data for 51% of the total audience. The reason for this is that Google Analytics can see demographics only if users have already shared it with them, in their Gmail account for example.

If you don't see this data, make sure you enable the Demographics and Interests reports.

In your Audience tab (Audience > Interests > Overview) you can see what your users are interested in:

In the same place, you can find info about which devices your users use, their behavior and of course their geolocation.

If your website's main audience are women aged 25-34, it doesn't necessarily mean that they are the best quality audience, and that you want to create campaigns to target them! While this might be the case, you need to look at engagement and conversion rates to see which audience has the best quality.

And here we realize that even though women aged 25-34 are the most common visitors, they're not the most profitable visitors. We actually want to target women aged 35-54, as they are far more likely to purchase your product.

Keep in mind that this data is informational, you should not base your decision on that only as it might show you only half of the picture.

Google Search Console

Google Search Console is a tool used to track organic searches that lead to your website, as well as help index all your pages organically in Google. If you have it linked to your Google Analytics account, then you can see the results directly there.

If you don't have Google Search Console, integrate it with your site and wait for a few days (or weeks, months) to gather enough data from your organic performance.

You might want to look at the searches which have a poor ranking position and a good number of impressions. These are likely the best bets for you to go for.

QUERIES	PAGES	COUNTRIES	DEVICES	SEARCH APPEARANCE	
Queries		Clicks	↓ Impressions	CTR	Position
organic juices		22	635	3.5%	6.8
organic juice		25	611	4.1%	5.4
organic cola		6	517	1.2%	14.4
organic drinks		10	481	2.1%	27.8
white tea		0	344	0%	58
organic soft drinks		3	320	0.9%	28.1
iced tea		0	262	0%	59.2
juices		3	260	1.2%	12.9
organic ginger beer		8	222	3.6%	5.5
organic drinks wholesale		1	215	0.5%	28.2
			Rows per page: 10 ▼	1-10 of 999	< >

Bing Webmaster Tools & Yandex Webmaster

The same tools and techniques in Google Search Console are also available in Bing Webmaster Tools. Yandex also offers a webmaster tool as well!

You also might take a look at Yandex Metrica, which is an analytics plugin similar to Google Analytics. It's free and often provides even more data than Google Analytics does, as well as a few other features here and there.

Google Analytics Site Search

If your website has a search option like this, you can see what people searched for in your Analytics account. Based on this data, you'll be able to see how people search and what they need from you. Use this to discover what problems your audience is trying to solve. When you've found these problems, tailor your ads to help solve their problems!

If you don't have a Google Analytics account, you can create one on the Analytics site. If you don't see any data in the Search Terms tab, make sure you've enabled the tracking of this data. There many other tools that can be used, and some of them are free like the ones shown above. You can also use paid tools (like Moz Keyword Explorer or SEMRush) and you can always get creative!

But back to Anya's Organics campaign. We're using all these tools to fill in our keywords list. When we've collected all search variations we'll have a large final list.

Detox Juice	Juice Cleanse	x Day Juice Cleanse	Organic Juices	Organic Soft Drinks	Organic Kombucha	Pressed Juice	Negatives
cold pressed detox juice	cold pressed juice cleanse	2 day Juice cleanse	cold pressed organic juices	cold pressed Soft Drinks	cold pressed Organic Kombucha	Organic pressed juice	juicer
detox juice california	juice cleanse california	3 day juice cleanse	Organic juices california	Organic Soft Drinks california	Organic Kombucha california	Pressed Juice california	vipe
Organic detox juice	Organic juice cleanse	5 day Juice cleanse	Organic juices delivery	Organic Soft Drinks delivery	Organic Kombucha delivery	Pressed Juice detox	recipes
detox juice delivery	juice cleanse delivery>	7 day juice cleanse	Organic juices online	Organic Soft Drinks online	Organic Kombucha online	Pressed Juice delivery	whole-foods
detox juice online	juice cleanse online	2 day Juice detox	order Organic juices	order Organic Soft Drinks	order Organic Kombucha	Pressed Juice online	dispenser
order detox juice	order juice cleanse	3 day Juice detox	buy Organic juices	buy Organic Soft Drinks	buy Organic Kombucha	order Pressed Juice	jobs
buy detox juice	buy juice cleanse	5 day juice detox	Best Organic juices	Best Organic Soft Drinks	Best Organic Kombucha	buy Pressed Juice	machine
Best detox juice	Best juice cleanse	7 day juice detox				Best Pressed Juice	wine

Chapter 4: Building A Google Ads Campaign

4.1 Deciding your advertising goals

Welcome to the most important chapter in our guide: how to structure a PPC campaign.

We'll start out by visiting with our imaginary client, Anya's Organic Juices, and helping them nail down their primary goal. Is it just more website traffic? Or is it sales? Do they have an app they want to download? Or is it just brand awareness and increasing visibility?

The campaign will look very different depending upon the goal. It'll target different keywords, use different PPC channels, and there will be totally different types of metrics to watch.

Anya's Organics wants to increase visibility & branding as they expand their operations across the West Coast, but most of all they want to increase sales from their new ecommerce store. Website traffic is a secondary concern: it's nice to see more visitors, but we want quality over quantity.

Because of this, we will use multiple strategies to target both goals: branding and sales. For branding, we'll use display campaigns & video campaigns. For sales, we'll use a search campaign, a shopping campaign, and also some remarketing.

Before you start a campaign, make sure you have these questions answered:

- What is my goal (why do I need Google Ads?)
- What is my monthly budget (how much am I willing to spend to accomplish my goal?)
- If my goal is sales, how much can I spend and still be profitable (cost per acquisition?)
- Where does my target audience live?
- What age & gender are my ideal audience?
- What topics are my ideal audience interested in?
- What is their economic demographic?
- Does my product require a lot of research before purchase, or is it an impulse buy?

Only after you have answers to all of these questions can you start setting up your Google Ads campaign. If you do it before you know these answers, you'll incur a lot of expense and no revenue.

4.2 Choosing the right PPC channel

Different channels work for different niches. We've seen clients that spent $60,000 a month on Facebook ads and got an ROI of 25%, but Google Ads just wouldn't work for them. We've seen other clients spend $30,000 a month on Google Ads with an ROI of 50%, but months of Facebook Ads would just not bring any sales.

The main difference between these two clients was that the first had a low cost product that many people would see on Facebook and purchase on impulse without researching. The second client had a high cost product which people researched on Google for months before purchasing.

But in the end, even if only one channel works for you, it doesn't mean you need to ignore the other. If Anya's Organics is doing amazingly on Google, but doesn't have a presence on Facebook, the company might not have a lot of trust. And trust is 99.99% of sales (that's a made up number, but we'll stake our reputation on it).

Test extensively. Patience is a virtue, since you shouldn't expect too many sales at the beginning as you spend to build your brand. Good upfront branding will pay back double in the end!

Start with Instagram if you're selling fashion. Facebook if you're selling funny t-shirts. Google Ads if you're selling trips to luxury resorts in Africa. And don't forget about Bing Ads if you're targeting the US.

4.3 Campaigns for brand awareness & visibility

Historically, branding has always been one of the most complicated types of campaigns to track. It takes a longer time to show results and it's difficult to associate specific results with the campaign. A branding campaign will create awareness, and people will know your name, but it doesn't necessarily bring you immediate sales.

Display campaigns

When you create a new campaign, Google Ads allows you to choose the goal for your campaign (we will choose brand awareness and reach) and it guides you in what settings you'll need to pick in order to be successful in this goal. To do this, go to your Google Ads Account > New Campaign > Display. You'll be given options to set which country you're targeting, and what budget and bidding strategy you're using. When choosing bidding strategy, I recommend focusing on Conversions and setting your bids manually.

Now, it's time to choose your audience! You have two options: either targeting users based upon their online

actions, or targeting specific websites based upon topics and keywords.

For a branding campaign, I recommend testing both options and determining which brings you better results. To choose your audience, I suggest starting with a Custom Intent campaign. A Custom Intent audience allows you to make a list of keywords your perfect customer uses. Based upon this list, you'll have an audience that is actively researching using the keywords you picked.

If you've got a list of websites that use Google AdSense and have a high volume of traffic, you can create an audience which only includes users visiting these websites. To do this, create your audience using Content Targeting > Placements.

If you'd rather target users based on their interests and habits, you can create an Affinity Audience. This gives us options for Anya's Organics like "Green Living Enthusiasts" and "Heath & Fitness Buffs".

Once your audience has been chosen, you can start creating your ads.

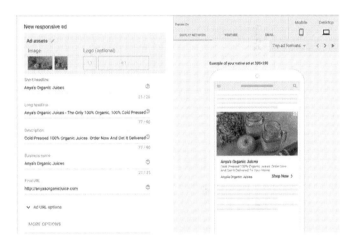

You'll be given a choice between creating Responsive ads, uploading display ads, and copying existing ads (if you have them). The difference between creating responsive ads and uploading your own is that for responsive ads, you just need to upload one image in 2 sizes. You'll also be able to add multiple titles and descriptions. Google Ads automatically adjusts the ad size, appearance, and format to fit available placements.

If you choose to upload your own ads, you'll need to

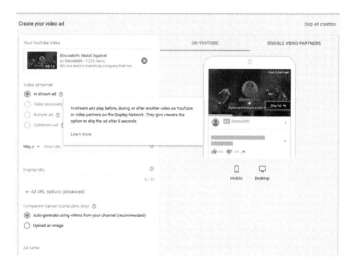

create images with text overlaid, for each display format you want to appear for. You can find the supported sizes and format in Google Ads documentation.

Your ads need to be memorable but not too pushy. You're not trying to annoy your users! Have a clear message, use short sentences, and explain the top benefits of your service.

Video Ads

Video advertising (usually on YouTube) is an excellent strategy for affordably raising awareness about your products. Setting up a YouTube campaign is easy. Go to your Google Ads account > New Campaign > Video and choose your campaign goal to be "Brand Awareness And Reach".

You can pick audiences the same way as the display campaign mentioned previously. You can additionally select specific YouTube channels you want to appear on, or choose which topics and keywords you'd like to appear for. Continue by choosing location, budgets, and bidding. For a video you bid per view (CPV) and on average, bids cost a few cents. For a branding ad, you'll only be able to select in-stream video format ads. In-stream ads are the videos that play before, during, and after another video. Users have the option to skip an ad after 5 seconds.

Make sure your video has a single main call-to-action. Don't forget that you're targeting users who have no idea who you are. Get their attention in the first 5 seconds (before they can skip). Don't use too much noise or annoyance: that's not how you want to get their attention.

Search Campaigns

All search engines support search campaigns: ads which appear in the SERPs (search engine results page). For branding campaigns, you don't want to target highly specific keywords or phrases. Target users searching for information and ideas: people who are still in the research phase rather than ready to purchase.

For Anya's Organic Juices branding campaign, we'll target users searching for "detox juice diet" and "benefits of cold pressed juices" rather than users searching for "where to buy organic juices near me".

Doing this will allow you to target a much broader audience. The CPC for general terms is usually cheaper, as well. You'll be the first brand they see during their research. Even if your audience is not ready to buy right away, when they're ready they'll have you in mind and likely go directly to your website. To get started, go to your Ads account > New Campaign > Search.

Your goal for a branding campaign is to get as much website traffic and visibility as possible. When you create the campaign, make sure it's Search campaign only. You don't want to have your Search and Display campaigns in the same place, so uncheck the box saying Display Network. It's recommended to keep them separate to analyze results and optimize campaigns based upon performance.

Now choose your targeted location, budget and bids. You don't have to create your extensions now. Create them later in the process: it will allow you to have more time to think about it.

Make sure when you define your targeting location carefully. Make sure you checked the box saying "People in or regularly in your targeted locations." I don't recommend choosing "people who show interest in your targeted location" as this usually results in poor quality traffic: Anya's Organics doesn't want to advertise juices for someone in Mongolia who has shown interest in

California, for example.

Now, all campaign settings have been created. For a search campaign, you'll have more ad groups. You can create them right away, or do it later. Remember the table we created in the keyword research chapter? Use the column title as your ad group title, and the phrases in the column as keywords.

Adding a plus in front of every word is the "broad match modifier" match type. This tells Google that you want to appear for searches that contain each keyword in any order.

For +buy +organic +juices, we'll appear for searches like "where I can buy organic juices" or "buy local organic juices".

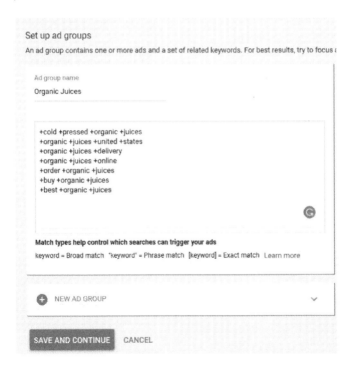

And finally, in a later chapter we'll talk more about how you can analyze your branding campaign's performance. But in short, one of the main ways to keep an eye out for success is through and increase in brand searches, organic traffic, and direct traffic to your website.

4.4 Campaigns for increasing sales

If you're already in the market and your website/brand is trustworthy, you probably want to focus on making sales. You should use a sales-focused strategy, rather than just branding.

Search campaign

When creating a sales-focused search campaign, you want to focus on searches that show an interest in purchasing your product. Your campaign should be specific and well-structured.

The setup itself is similar to search campaigns for branding purpose, but you want to focus on conversion and leads rather than website traffic. From the beginning you pick a different goal: sales if you have an ecommerce website, or leads if you have a service-based site.

Remember the branding campaign for Anya's Organics? We wanted to target users searching for educational info about cold pressed juice. Now, for their sales campaign, we want users searching for "buy organic juices online" or "the best place to buy organic cold pressed juices".

Make sure you have Analytics tracking all your leads/

sales, and track all the phone calls both from ads and from the website.

Shopping campaigns

Shopping campaigns show great results for ecommerce & retail websites. The primary benefit is that users see the product images, price and description before clicking. This means you only pay for clicks from users who know what to expect.

The limitation is that Shopping campaigns are not available in all countries.

To create a Shopping campaign, create a product feed with all included info required to be eligible. The fields you need to have depend on what type of product you're advertising. You can find the list of all Product Feed Specifications and the format of your data within Google's documentation.

Your next step is creating a Google Merchant Center account. Add all your basic business information, verify your URL and add all Tax & Shipping information.

After this, upload your spreadsheet in the Products tab

> Feeds > (+)New Feed. You can only choose one country and one language per feed.

After this, you'll be able to see how many of your products have errors and what should be changed to fix it. You can re-upload the document once it's fixed.

The image below is how your nightmare might look like. There's no easy way around this: it's not an easy process. Some ecommerce software services like Shopify help automate the process, allowing you to connect the website's product database with your Merchant account. The benefit of this is that your data is always updated.

United States, English

File pre-processing: Completed - 864 valid / 1685 processed
Basic product data completeness and correctness

DOWNLOAD REPORT

^ 900 errors, 1105 warnings

⌄ 97 ERROR: Encoding problem (double UTF8 encoding) in attribute: description.

⌄ 1 ERROR: Encoding problem (double UTF8 encoding) in attribute: title.

⌄ 3 ERROR: Insufficient product identifiers: Missing two out of three attributes [GTIN, brand, mpn].

⌄ 4 ERROR: Invalid GTIN value.

⌄ 328 ERROR: This value must be one of the values stated in the data feed instructions for attribute: age group.

⌄ 466 ERROR: This value must be one of the values stated in the data feed instructions for attribute: gender.

⌄ 1 ERROR: Unknown 'google product category' value.

⌄ 39 WARNING: Invalid or missing recommended attribute: description.

⌄ 10 WARNING: Invalid or missing recommended attribute: image link.

⌄ 1056 WARNING: Product identifiers provided but 'identifier_exists' set to false..

Remarketing campaigns

Remarketing campaigns allow you to show your ads to defined audiences of users who've already visited your site. You can separate users based on their behavior (converters vs non-converters), for users that visited a specific page on your site, are from a specific region, how many pages they visited, or time spent reading your articles.

You'll need to create your audience in Analytics. Your audience needs at least 100 unique users before it starts running, or 1000 users for a video or search remarketing campaign.

First, allow Analytics to collect remarketing information in Settings > Tracking info > Data Collections. Make sure Remarketing is on.

To create your audience, go to Settings > Audience Definition > Audiences and make sure your Google Ads account is linked to Analytics.

Once you do that, you'll have your first audience created: All Users.

As your Google Ads is already linked to your Analytics account, your Audience will be imported so you'll be able to find it easily within your account.

The All Users audience is useful if you have a new campaign, with no sales and an amount of users less than 100. Otherwise, you want to create an audience that excludes those who already purchased from you.

It's very annoying when you already purchased from a brand, but the ads continue following you. To avoid users being annoyed, and spending your budget needlessly, create a new audience that excludes converters: go to +New Audience.

Either create a custom audience or pick from existing options. Creating a new audience will give you more choices. You can see all your filters now. To create an audience that excludes all conversions, go to Conditions and exclude users with more than one transaction or more than one goal completion.

Now, name your audience and it's ready to be used!

There are 4 campaign types you can use your remarketing list in:

- Display Remarketing
- Dynamic Remarketing
- Video Remarketing
- Remarketing Lists for Search Ads (RLSA)

Each of these campaign types allows you to connect with your previous customers. The benefit is that you can personalize your message based on user behavior.

Display Remarketing

You will need to create a display campaign. The process is the same as creating a branding display campaign. The difference is in the audience. Choose your audience as remarketing. You'll see a list of all remarketing audiences that you've created in your Analytics account. Choose the one you need. If you have multiple audiences with different audiences, create an ad group for each of them. This will allow you to personalize your ads and messages. When creating ads, remember that the users you're targeting are already familiar with your service. Don't be salesy: try to be creative and personal.

A Dynamic Remarketing campaign allows you to create display ads showing the exact product the user saw on your website. It will include a title and a description. To create one of these, you'll need a product or service feed. If you're a retailer, you'll need to use your product feed from Google Merchant Center (the same one you're using for a Shopping campaign). Follow the steps of creating a simple display remarketing campaign. Below the Budget tab, you'll see additional settings. Open it, look for dynamic ads, and check the box that says "Use a data feed for personalized ads". If you don't have your feed already uploaded to Google Ads, just choose your business type.

If you do have your feed ready to go, you'll be asked to select it. Then, in the Audiences tab, choose a remarketing list (I suggest creating a list with all users except those that already converted).

Now we need to create our ads. The process is the same as creating normal display ads, except now we'll be able to preview the products from our feed. If you're products are not shown yet, don't worry. Sometimes it takes a while for Google to crawl all your images in Merchant Center.

Video Remarketing

To be able to create a video remarketing list, you'll need to have at least 1000 users in it. Just create a normal video campaign, and choose the audience from one you created in Analytics (with over 1000 users).

Remarketing Lists for Search Ads (RLSA)

This one is an addition to a simple search campaign. It lets you personalize the ads and bids for those who've already visited your website while searching on Google.

Let's say someone visited Anya's Organics but didn't purchase anything. Here, we'll choose that as your visitor continues their research you'll bid 2x your normal bid to make sure you're always on top of all their search results.

To add this list to your search campaign, go to the search campaign to change > Audiences > click the pen!

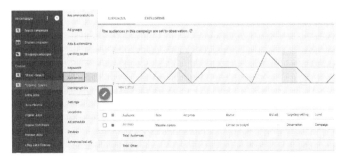

Either add the audience to target only those users, or

choose the audience for observation.

If you choose "Targeting" it allows you to show ads to your remarketing audience ONLY. So you can personalize all the messaging with the idea that they've already visited your site, and maybe try sending them to a different landing page.

If you choose Observation, you'll still be able to adjust your ads and bids based on the audience, but the campaign will include all users searching for your search terms. And, same as for video ads, you need at least 1000 unique users in your audience before you can start the campaign.

4.5 Campaign structure and naming

Now that we know which campaigns we need, and how to set them up, we need to think more about our account structure. It's important to do it correctly, since the more organized the campaign the better we'll be able to optimize later on.

While doing keyword research, we've already completed half of the job!

First, we decide what type of campaign we want to start with. For Anya's Organic Juices we want to have a Shopping campaign, Search campaign and a Dynamic remarketing campaign. We want to keep them all separated. Each will have a separate budget.

If you target different regions and maybe have different budgets for each, you might want to have 2 of each campaign: Shopping Campaign CAD and Shopping Campaign USA, for example.

Also, if we want to create a campaign with brand

searches only (for searches like "anya's organic juices") you want to separate it from the main search campaign. The reason is that a brand campaign will always be 10x more successful compared to non-brand campaigns. For the simple fact that if someone searches directly for your brand name they're already much more likely to convert compared to a general researcher.

If you've got a product that you want to gain more attention, with a separate budget, you also want a separate campaign. Let's use Kombucha as an example.

Ok, so, now we have 5 final campaigns:
- Shopping Campaign
- Dynamic Remarketing Campaign
- Brand - Search
- Kombucha - Search
- Organic Juice - Search

As shown in the example above, their names should be short and clear. It's like creating product category on your website. Never use names that are too generic like "Campaign 1" or it will be a nightmare to remember which campaign does what. Now that we have them, we need to name our ad groups. When we did our exercise in the Keywords Research campaign we already did that. So our final version will be close to this:
- Shopping Campaign (campaign name)
  - Shopping Ads (ad group)
- Dynamic Remarketing Campaign (campaign name)
  - Dynamic Remarketing Ads (ad group)
- Brand - Search (campaign name)
  - Anya's Organic
- Kombucha - Search (campaign name)

- Kombucha
- Organic Juice - Search (campaign name)
  - Juice Cleanse
  - Detox Juice
  - x Day Juice Cleanse
  - Organic Juices
  - Organic Soft Drinks
  - Pressed Juice

The ad group name should represent the keywords targeted within it. In the "Pressed Juice" ad groups you want only keywords containing the words pressed and juice, like +buy +organic +pressed +juice or +pressed +juice +delivery.

Beside helping you track everything better, it will also help improve your Quality Score and relevancy. In the end, the better your campaign is organized, the less you'll pay for your clicks and the higher your revenue will be.

4.6 Ad and extension creation

The ad itself is very important as this is the first thing the user sees before interacting with you. Whether we're talking about social media ads, search, or display, all ads should follow the same rules. One of them is: be respectful to the users. Have nice visuals, clear message, good grammar, quality images and a clear call-to-action.

You'd think it goes without saying, but just remember the ads from just six or seven years ago. Some advertisers are still trying to use those old techniques, but thankfully they're now forbidden on most advertising platforms. But in short, your ads can be disapproved for:

- Poor splling or gramar
- !!!Too many exclamation points!!!
- WORDS WRITTEN IN CAPS
- CLICK HERE
- No emojis :(
- youcannotdothiseither

To write great ads, there are some simple steps.

Include your main features and benefits. What makes you better than your competitor? Do you have anything unique that you provide? What problems does your service help with? What does your customer gain by choosing you?

Add a call to action (CTA). What is the final action you want your users to take when they land on your website? We'll choose something like "Get 100% Organic Juice" or maybe "Detox Your Body With Cold Pressed Juices". The last one is both a benefit and a CTA. You want to be smart about your message as you're limited by the number of characters you are allowed to use.

Avoid repetition! Sometimes, when you don't have any inspiration (or maybe your products don't really have that many special benefit) it might be hard to come up with great copy. We often see ads that say the same thing in the title, description and extensions. And I'm telling you, it looks bad! You're already limited by the number of characters, so don't waste this space. If you have a special offer, use it in the ad! Either it's "Free Shipping" or "10% Off The First Order". Let people know even before they go to your website.

A/B test! There is no single ad structure that works the best for everyone. You have to keep testing different ads and see how they perform. All ad groups should have at least 2-3 ads with slightly different messaging. Once you get around 100 clicks, see how different the performance for each of them is.

Find which one has a better CTR (click-through-rate). Look at conversion rate. Which ad gave you move leads? There are ads that have a very high CTR but users aren't necessarily the same quality as another with lower CTR.

In the ads, use the wording your audience uses to search for your service. Looking at your search terms report, you might see that Anya's Organics users like the phrase "Best Organic Remedy Kombucha" so why not use it as your title?

As an example, this can be our ad 1 (the actual ad text is in the highlighted area):

Best Organic Remedy Kombucha | 100% Californian Organic Drink
[Ad] www.anyasorganic.com/kombucha
100% Californian Organic Kombucha. Order Now And Get It Delivered To Your Home!
No Additives · 100% Organic Juice · No Artificial Sugars · No Preservatives
Types: Body Booters, Cleanse Juice, Organic Fruit Juices, Organic Sparkling, Organic Soft Drinks

How We Do It
Our fresh fruit is sourced directly from 100% organic growers.

Gift Card
Give a healthy 100% Californian and Organic gift to a friend.

Benefits
Learn more about why organic is good for you and our environment

Wholesale
Your customers will love our delicious, healthy juices & drinks.

And ad 2 can be this:

Anya's Organic Kombucha | 10% Off On All Repeat Orders
[Ad] www.anyasorganic.com/kombucha
The Only 100% Organic, 100% Cold Pressed and 100% Californian. Order Now Online!
No Additives · 100% Organic Juice · No Artificial Sugars · No Preservatives
Types: Body Booters, Cleanse Juice, Organic Fruit Juices, Organic Sparkling, Organic Soft Drinks

How We Do It
Our fresh fruit is sourced directly from 100% organic growers.

Gift Card
Give a healthy 100% Californian and Organic gift to a friend.

Benefits
Learn more about why organic is good for you and our environment

Wholesale
Your customers will love our delicious, healthy juices & drinks.

Ad extensions

As you can see in the example above, the actual ad text is just a half of the job (or even less). To make your ad stand out and have more visibility you need to create ad extensions. Here are some of the most common:

- Sitelink extension - Show additional links from your website
- Callout extension - Add some additional benefits of your products
- Structured snippet extension - Add some specifics of your products (brand names, destinations)
- Call extension - Your phone number
- Message extension - Let people text you directly from the ad
- Location extension - shows business information (address, working hours)
- Affiliate location extension - Show affiliate location
- Price extension - Show prices of your products and services
- App extension - Add a link to your app
- Promotion extension - Use it for special offers

4.7 Keyword match types

Keyword Match Types help control which searches your ads will appear for. It tells Google how flexible you want to be.

A keyword is the word you choose to target in your Google Ads account. A search term is the exact words or phrases the customer enters while searching on a search engine. These are different: don't confuse them!

There are 5 main types of keywords.

Broad match - Ads will show for for synonyms, misspellings, and related searches. So, if your keyword is *organic juices*, your ads could show for *buy cold pressed juices*. Symbol: no symbols added.

Broad match modifier - These ads will show only for searches that include your keywords (or close variations, no matter in what order. So, if your keyword is *+organic +juice +delivery*, your ads will appear for the search term *home delivery organic juice*. Symbol: Plus sign, for example +keyword.

Phrase match - These ads will show only for searches that match a phrase (or close variations). It might have words before and after the phrase you target. So, if your keyword is *"detox juice delivery"* your ads will appear for searches like *best detox juice delivery california*. Symbol: "keyword"

Exact match - Ads will show on searches with the exact words or phrases you're targeting (or close variations). So if your keyword is *[buy organic juice]*, your ad will appear for someone searching for *buy organic juices*. Symbol: [keyword]

Negative match - Ads will show on searches that don't include negative keywords. If you sell organic juice, but you don't do wholesale orders, you'll add the keyword *-wholesale* as a negative, and if someone searches for *wholesale organic juices*, your ads won't show up. Symbol: -keyword

Because broad match keywords don't give you much control over which searches you appear for, we usually don't recommend using them. Use only when you have very low search volume or very limited niche.

Some other notes:

There is no need to add keywords in both lower case and upper case. For Google Ads, *+Organic +Juice* keyword is the same as *+organic +juice*.

Your keywords cannot contain symbols like: % ! @*.

If you're adding keywords for a display campaign, they'll be seen as broad match only.

Close variations include misspellings, singular forms, plural forms, acronyms, stems, abbreviations, and accents.

You can learn more about keyword match types at Google's support site. We recommend reading through them, as they tend to change from time to time.

4.8 Budgets & bidding

As we know, online advertising works on the principle that you pay when someone clicks on your ad (pay-per-click) and this is based on an auction. Let's say that five companies want to appear for the search term "organic juices delivery". Each will bid on this keyword. A bid is the maximum amount you are willing to pay for that click. Whoever pays more gets a higher position. The higher position you have on a search engine, the more people will see your ad.

The decision on how much you want to spend for a click is NOT totally up to you. The reason is that your competitors are already there, and have set an average of how much it costs to be on top of the search results.

Your cost per click should be competitive, in order for

people to see your ads.

While doing keyword research you can usually get an idea of how much a click should cost for your keywords. For both Google Ads and Bing, you can do it from the Keywords Planner.

This number will not be our final bid, but gives an idea of where to start and what to expect.

As our CPC is different based on the bids of our competitors, in the exact moment someone searches our CPC will vary as well.

We can have different strategies for our bidding strategy. We can pick between manually bidding per ad group or even per keywords, based on their importance to us. It can take more time to analyze each keyword's performance and choose the best bids for each, but the effort can save us a lot of money.

Or, we can go with automated bidding strategies developed by the search engine's software. The benefits are that you won't need to choose your bids. The downside is that you won't be able to control your CPC and, based on our experience, a click that should cost $2 can turn into $15. You can still chose the maximum you want to pay, or you can choose how much you want to pay for conversion. But, we don't suggest it. Use it only if you have a large amount of campaigns and you don't have someone to look at the performance regularly.

If you decide to use manual bidding strategy, you can

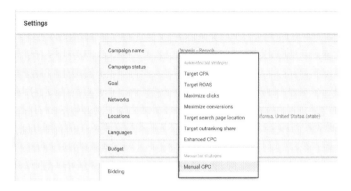

add an option to add a bid adjustment based on device, location, audience, demographics and even household income (for US only).

If you've decided that you want to bid higher for users that have already visited your website, you can import your audience from Analytics (as we previously discussed in the remarketing section) and add a bid adjustment of +30% to make sure that you appear on top for all users that are already familiar with your business.

Also, if you are targeting a bigger country like the US, some areas might be more competitive than others. With the same bid, you might be the first position in Arkansas, but only the fourth for California. In this case you add bid adjustment to make sure you have a good position even in more competitive areas.

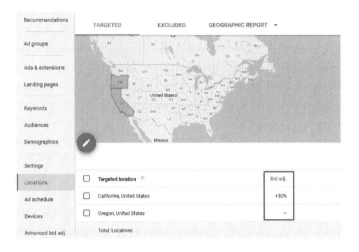

Don't forget that when you set up a new campaign, you assume which bidding strategy and which CPC is the best for you, but you never know for sure. Once the campaign has some clicks, make sure you update and optimize based on performance, conversion rate and average position.

Also, don't forget that you can lower your CPC by having a high Quality Score. The better the user experience is and the more closely targeted your campaign is, the lower your CPC will be.

Monthly Budgets

Now that we know the approximate cost per click, we'll need to decide our monthly budget.

Let's say that Anya's Organics estimated CPC is $2.50. We must calculate the amount we can spend in order for a sale to be profitable.

If your average revenue per conversion is $100, but your built-in overhead (besides advertising expenses) is $40. Your margin = revenue-expenses, or $60.

Now that we know the margin, we know how much we can spend on advertising per order. If our average CPC is $2.50, we need to make a sale every 24 clicks to break even (24*2.50=60). However, Anya's Organics wants to turn a profit (don't we all?) so they decide they need to make a sale every 20 clicks (for a $10 profit per sale).

So we want to spend a maximum of $50 on advertising per sale. This might not happen right away as it's a competitive niche. So we'll need to test the campaign, see what works best, and then work on getting the desired cost per conversion.

It's also essential to understand our desired conversion rate. To calculate it, divide conversions by the number of interactions with your ad. To get a sale every 20 clicks we need a conversion rate of 5%.

In the end, you will also want to know your ROI. Calculate this with the formula below:

ROI = (Revenue - Total Cost) / Total Cost

In our case that would be ($100 -($40+50)/ (40+50) *100% = 10/90*100% = 11.1%

In the equation below we have:
Our initial number:

Revenue per order = $100
Expenses = $40
Margin = $60

Our desired advertising results:
Advertising expenses = $50
Profit = $10
Conversion rate = 5%
ROI = 11.1%

How many sales a month do you want to get? Say you want to start with 10 sales per month. If your cost per sale is around $50, your monthly budget should be $50 *10 = $500/mo.

Starting Budgets

If you were to ask me the most common question we get when we onboard a new client - especially those who are fresh to the digital advertising scene - then I'd immediately have an answer for you. It's "how much do I need to spend on Google Ads?"

You probably came here looking for a satisfying, definite answer. Sorry to have to disappoint you...but there's no universally applicable answer for every advertiser. No magic number that works for every company. But, the good news is, there's a perfect number for you, and there's a few ways to find that number.

Coming from a purely anecdotal, experiential perspective, we can draw some generalizations that are applicable to most campaigns. From Discosloth's experience, most small businesses don't start seeing any results at all until at least $1000 per month in ad spend, and they really only start seeing amazing results at around $3000 per month. Some of the most successful businesses in our client base spend upwards of $50,000 per month. (And, of course, this is digital ads only - spending on SEO and content is additional).

The right amount to spend on Google Ads depends on a few factors: your revenue, the competitiveness of your industry, and perhaps above all your profit margin. It's more of a business model decision than an advertising decision, so in order to answer this question for yourself you'll need to know the details of your finances inside and out.

In the end, it's all about ROI. We make a big deal about this. Discosloth literally only exists in order to help our clients make money - so we only encourage a Google Ads campaign if it's profitable for you. And usually, if a campaign is profitable, it can be scaled accordingly. But you didn't come here to listen to us jaw on about business models and revenue, even though it's really important. You actually want to know how much other people spend on Google Ads, right?

I'll go through a few typical use cases to give you an idea of how much other people are spending.

Although these are anonymized, for the purposes of the article let's assume that these cases are all located in the United States, all are profitable businesses, and all have been using Google Ads as a primary driver of sales and leads for at least a year.

Health Clinic - $70,000 per year

For the first use case, let's look at a privately owned local health clinic in a Midwestern state. Because healthcare is a costly industry, they've got a relatively high lifetime value per customer, so they can afford the expensive bids in this niche. This clinic spends a little over $70,000 per year (or around $6,000 a month) on Google Ads. Not only does this bring them significant revenue, but it also lets them run hiring campaigns when they need some extra help.

Boutique Children's Clothing Ecommerce Store - $14,000 per year

For our second use case, let's look at a small ecommerce store selling boutique kid's clothes. While the client also has a brick and mortar store, they use their online store to serve customers in other states and in order to promote their brand in the area. This small business client spends around $14,000 per year (or around $1,150 a month) on Google Ads. Since they're a small business, their cash flow limits how much they're able to spend but if they had the budget they'd be able to triple or quadruple their ad spend and still be profitable.

Luxury Travel Company - $375,000 per year

For our third use case, let's look at a mid-sized luxury hospitality company based in the US. This company has revenues around $20 million a year, and attributes almost

40% of that to Google Ads. This company spends around $375,000 per year, or $32,000 a month on digital advertising - an amount that generates around $8 million in sales. At a profit margin of 15%, this means that their $375,000 in ad cost gains them around $1.2 million in profits, or a net return of $825,000 per year.

It's also probably worth looking over our PPC metrics section, which helps you understand how to measure your paid advertising metrics in order to budget for a profitable campaign.

Of course, it's important to remember that everyone's idea budget is different. In a perfect world, we'd be able to spend $1 to make $1000, but until then we'll have to do the math and buckle down to find what number works the best for each of us. Having a baseline to work from is useful, so use some of the numbers in this article to help decide whether your Google Ads budget is in the right ballpark.

Chapter 5: Conversion Optimization & UI/UX

One of the most important things to understand about creating a profitable PPC campaign is that success doesn't just depend on the campaign. There are a lot of factors in play. One of the most crucial is knowing how to convert visitors once they visit your site.

You can have the best Google Ads campaign in the world, but if your site sucks, you won't make any profit.

We'll take a brief look at various aspects of your website which need to be addressed in order to see great results from PPC.

5.1 Landing pages

If you've spent any amount of time in the online marketing world, you've doubtless heard a lot about landing pages. But don't believe everything you read online. One of the most common myths, usually perpetuated by inbound marketing companies & landing page generators, is that you need to have a separate page for each targeted keyword in order to get high engagement and sales. Some people even tell you to create new websites with new domains. But this is an outdated strategy and won't help your sales. Why? Because Google calls these Doorway pages and they are against Google's policies.

In the world of inbound marketing, a landing page is created for a singular purpose: gaining a conversion. There is usually a simple, clear CTA (call-to-action) which directs users to an action like downloading something or submitting a form. These pages are usually ridiculous. They're not made to add value for users. The only purpose is to create a high-pressure sales environment that encourages the user to BUY NOW a thousand times. This funnel-loading tactic discourages careful research, and tries to prevent users from leaving to find some other better product. Often, they'll even use mouseover scripts to sense when a user is leaving a page, and then flash a last-minute popup to try to retain a user.

Not all landing pages are evil, of course. But the best landing pages are the ones that aren't there to sell, but to create a good experience for the audience. Google prioritizes pages that provide real value to a user: either by being educational, entertaining, informative, or useful in some manner.

A landing page, also known as a destination page, is the page through which the user enters your website. As simple as that. You can even see all the landing pages in a Google Analytics report: just go to Behaviour > Site Content > Landing Pages

It's an important part of your campaign because it's the second thing the user sees after he clicks on the ad. The user will decide if he trusts you within the first 2 seconds he lands on the page. The initial first impression will determine in his mind if you're professional and if he's ready to work with you and buy your services or products.

The landing page experience is part of Quality Score (for channels like Google Ads). This means that the higher the score is, the lower your CPC (cost-per-click) will be. A good landing page experience is directly correlated with how useful & relevant the user finds the page (some of the metrics to look at are bounce rate and average session duration).

So what makes a successful landing page?

- Good design
- Fast load speed
- Mobile-friendly responsive HTML
- Easy-to-read and informative content
- Nice pictures (professional quality)
- An easy way of buying or signing up for something

The more you care about good design and good content, the lower your marketing costs will be...and as a bonus, you'll have a higher conversion rate.

For one of our clients, we A/B tested their existing homepage design with a new & improved design. The results were amazing. In just 2 weeks the following metrics were improved:

- The conversion rate for the new home page was 28.6% higher than the old one
- The bounce rate was 19.8% lower
- Time on page was 6% higher
- Users were 15.4% more likely to click on the CTA (call-to-action) on the top banner

During our analysis of this client's website performance, we realized that homepage conversion was a problem. The primary purpose of their website was signing up new users for their web app, and we thought we could improve the conversion rate for this process.

The current website was built on an outdated Wordpress template. It was narrow, non-responsive, and felt too corporate. The images felt like stock images, and there were 5 calls-to-action immediately visible.

We redesigned the homepage to feel wider, newer, and responsive for mobile devices. Instead of stock images, we added high-quality photos that felt natural and authentic. We also removed distractions, simplifying the site down to 1 primary call-to-action.

Our hypothesis was that these strategies— simplifying, modernizing, and defining the message— would increase conversion rates. We decided to test the new page concurrently with the old in order to prove our hypothesis. We set up Google Analytics experiments (you can access this by going to Reports > Behavior > Experiments) to set up an A/B test. The old page's home was on the original link, and the new page's home was on a new URL (not indexed by Google) called /homepage.

You can also use Google's free analytics tool called Optimize. Other tools to consider are screen recording apps like Hotjar, for watching user behavior on site. Yandex Metrica also offers a great free alternative to Hotjar.

We set the experiment to run for 2 weeks. We directed 25% of the site traffic to our A/B experiment. Of these, half were shown the new page and half the old page. Then, after seeing good results in the first 6 days, we started sending 50% of the site traffic to the new page. The first 6 days of the test saw a conversion rate for the new home page that was 101.22% higher than the old one. Bounce rate improved by 44.71%. The average number of pages people visited per session improved by 11.03%. The CTA (call to action) click-through rate on the homepage improved by 25.63%.

We made a few small adjustments for search indexing in the content of the page, and published the page, making it live for 100% of visitors. The result was a drastic increase of product signups for the client.

Learning how to track performance can be the difference between a mediocre marketing campaign and an amazing marketing campaign. That's why the skills covered in this chapter are so important: being able to report and accurately detail every dollar spent on a campaign definitely helps a marketer succeed with clients and other departments within their companies.

5.2 Friendly design and interface

Good design is essential for your website. Good design is not subjective: there are clear factors that go into a good vs. bad design. It's not enough to just use a modern template. A great website requires all aspects of design to work together in a cohesive manner.

Clean, simple layout. Minimalism isn't just a fad. It's an intentional design choice that removes the distractions of a cluttered design in order to place an emphasis on the most important parts. Using appropriate amounts of negative space is not a waste: by isolating the most important elements, you're drawing the eye of the user where the most important content is. Make it simple for the user to understand where they need to click next. Offering a dozen options isn't good: it's better to have one or two buttons.

Consistent branding & color choice. Every part of your website should look like it belongs to your brand. That means using the same font, colors, styling, and design language throughout the entire site. If your company already has an established branding guide, you can use this consistently throughout your site. If not, spend some time developing your "look & feel". Look and feel is one of the most underrated aspects of a brand. While many are quick to dismiss it as trivial, it's an unavoidable part of the success of a website. A website that even looks a couple years old and has an outdated feel has already lost a level of trust within the first few seconds of the user visiting the page.

Voice & messaging. What attitude does your brand have? Whether it's playful, formal, professional, funny, or sarcastic is up to you. But it needs to be consistent, and this shows in things like your call-to-actions, page headings, content, colors, and design. For example, if you're a medical consultant, you probably don't want to have a sarcastic tone. You want to convey utmost trust and professionalism, so you pick strong colors like blue and white, you write clear and formal English, you avoid using too many exclamation points, and choose professional photography. However, if you're a skateboard shop, choosing the formal tone of the medical consultant would be a disaster. You can be irreverent, sarcastic, and edgy. Choose black and red colors, grungy fonts, abstract street photography, and use all the slang you want.

Photography. Professional photography is essential for the most engaging websites. Just using a 24-megapixel camera doesn't make your photography good: make sure that you've got a high level of quality throughout your images. Composition, lighting, clarity, and presentation is of the utmost importance.

5.3 Conversion optimization

Conversion optimization could have an entire chapter to itself, but it can essentially be boiled down into one simple statement: make it easy.

Everything should be easy and effortless for the customer. Easy to learn about the product, easy to navigate, easy to convert, easy to pay.

Essentially, the more steps you add in between the user first seeing your ad and your final conversion goal, the less likely the user will be to follow through. So keep it simple. Here are some tips to keep in mind:

- Make the call-to-action prominent and clear
- Show plenty of information and images about your product

- Make sure your benefits are clearly shown (free shipping, guarantees, etc)
- Make your conversion goal easy to see (simple, straightforward buttons or forms)
- Offer multiple payment methods (both credit cards and PayPal, for example)
- Make sure your site is very fast.
- Make sure your site works on all devices.

Does site speed affect conversion? The answer: absolutely. Approximately every additional second that a site takes to load can result in up to a 7% reduction in conversions. Numbers vary widely according to your niche and your platform, but you should aim for a page load speed of under 2 seconds.

For example, a few years ago Walmart decided their site wasn't fast enough. After some testing and research, they found out that for every 1 second of improvement they experienced up to a 2% increase in conversions. For every 100 ms of improvement, they grew incremental revenue by up to 1%. That is considerable, especially when applied at scale.

Chapter 6: Google Ads Management & Optimization

6.1 How does ongoing optimization make a difference?

We have our campaign ready to go. Congrats! But it's not over yet. The most important part of the job starts now.

When we create a campaign, we create the foundation. This foundation is based on our research, on our ideas of how people search, and hopefully on some existing data (which isn't always available with new websites). We don't know exactly what will work and give us sales. So where do we start?

We get this question a lot. And it's not an easy answer. There is no way that anyone has a perfect campaign the first day after setup, or even the first week! Once you have a running campaign, patience is a virtue. It might be a few days or a few months after the campaign starts (based on volume & budget) to gather enough data to get a cursory idea of how the campaign is performing.

How to keep your campaign optimized:

Find the average cost-per-click for keywords. But since you don't know what bidding strategy your competitors use, you'll need to adjust bidding based upon how much competition there is, and the average position you want to maintain.

Targeted keywords have been set up, but as we've learned, keywords are not search terms. You must constantly monitor the search term report. See which terms you appear for, which aren't correct (add these as negative keywords), and determine which you want to target more specifically. Once you find these, add them as a keyword. You can now adjust bids for it and track separately from others.

At the beginning, you set up 2-3 ads to test wording variations. Once you gather data, see which have better CTR (click-through-rate) and better conversion rates. Pause the ones that perform poorly, and create new variations to get even better performance. Find specific phrases searchers use. Use these in the ad text.

Looking at the keyword view, track your Quality Score. A score of 7-10 means users find your ads relevant to the keywords, and they find your landing page useful. If you have a low Quality Score, see what's missing.

If ad relevance is bringing your average down, try updating your ad wording. Make sure it's highly relevant to the keywords you're targeting. If you're targeting users searching for Kombucha, you don't want to ads to say Best Organic Juices sending traffic to a general page. You want these users to see an ad saying Best Organic Kombucha which sends them to Kombucha drink page.

We'll talk more about how to use Google Analytics in the next chapter. But a valuable Analytics feature for optimization is tracking user engagement.

Compare bounce rate, time on page, and pages per session with the other channels that bring traffic to your site (like organic search, social, or direct traffic). Compare between all campaigns & ad groups. Do users searching for Juice Cleanse have a higher engagement compared to those that searched for Pressed Juices?

Check your performance per device. Do users that came from a mobile device have a better conversion rate, CTR or engagement? Or does desktop perform better?

While targeting mobile, make sure your website is easy to use from a mobile device. Is it easy to read and easy to purchase? If desktop has a higher conversion rate, maybe you need to add a bid adjustment for it, or perhaps you want to lower mobile bids by 15%? While optimizing the campaign, asking yourself questions is the best you can do! If the website is just not that great, you might want to work on improving the look, usability or wording. Even the best campaign can't help a crappy website.

If that's the case, see if there is something different in your offer, ads or anything else which might need to be changed. See what the competitors offer for these products.

Do they have a better offer for Pressed Juices compared to you? Or is it something else?

6.2 Multi-channel attribution

A sale doesn't usually happen through a single click. No one sees your ad once and decides right away they want to buy from you. The internet makes it easy for us to research, read reviews and see multiple options before anyone decides that they want to purchase from you.

Before you decide if a campaign is performing well or if a specific channel is bringing you good results, you have to look at the user's journey.

Let's say you have a very high conversion rate for your brand campaign. Are these only users that know you from somewhere else, and they just Googled your name right away? Or did they research you for a week or two before they finally decide they trust your brand?

Maybe they searched for "where to buy kombucha". They checked your website along with some competitors. Then they decided to narrow down their search for "organic kombucha". They find you organically, then later they Google your brand name directly, click on the ad and purchase! And yes, that's the actual path someone used to make 2 purchases.

Should all the credit go to the brand search, because it was the term they searched before purchasing? No, because if they wouldn't see your ad for "where to buy kombucha"in the first place, they might never have found your website and wouldn't consider buying from you. You can see this data in both Google Ads and Analytics. Online advertising has an amazing benefit compared to traditional media. It allows you to see everything. We should take advantage of this feature, and gather as much as data as we're allowed to before making advertising decisions. We'll learn more about analyzing data in the next chapter.

Chapter 7: Measuring Google Ads Results

7.1 Analyzing your Google Ads performance

Analytics is one of the most crucial parts of your campaign's performance. If you don't track your results and adjust your campaigns based on data, you are going to waste so much money it's not even funny. It's a lot to talk about here (we could write a whole book explaining how to measure things) so we'll try to be short and to the point. To make sure you analyze your data correctly, there are a few tools you should use that will help with your data-driven decisions. But the main one to start with is Google Analytics.

Google Analytics is a web analytics tool created by Google that allows you to track your website traffic. It's the most commonly used web analytics tool out there, and you can use it for free. Analytics is a very important tool, but underused by the majority of businesses.

It allows you to:

- See your website traffic in real time (Reports > Real Time)
- See more details about your audience. See things like:

demographics, interests, geo location, the device and browser they use and more (Reports > Audience)

- You can also track user engagement, which gives you a grasp of the quality of the traffic you're getting. (Reports > Audience)
- Analyze your Google Ads performance per campaign, search queries, destination URLs and more. (Reports > Acquisition > Google Ads)
- You can also link your search console to Analytics and see data about your organic traffic. (Reports > Acquisition > Search Console)
- Analyze user behavior on your website. Here you can see info about site speed, see searches that happened on the website, see all the events you are tracking and the performance for each of your pages. (Reports > Behaviour)
- See which channels are sending you traffic. (Reports > Acquisition)
- You can create your own, customized reports and create something that shows only the data you need. (Customisation > Custom Reports)
- And last, but not least, you can see all of your conversion data. If you have an ecommerce website, you can see which products sold, order value and other info about user shopping behaviour. (Reports > Conversions > E-commerce > Shopping Behaviour)

If you are advertising via social media, email marketing or any other channels where you want to track your campaign separately from organic (unpaid) traffic, make sure you add UTM tracking. UTM tracking is a code added at the end of links that give Analytics more information about your campaigns. Search for Google's URL Builder to create this. The final URL you'll use in your campaign will look something like this:

https://www.anyasorganic.com/?
utm_source=facebook&utm_medium=cpc&utm_campaign=o
rganic_juice_promo.

It will tell Analytics that the traffic is coming from a Facebook campaign (utm_source=facebook), it's from a paid campaign (utm_medium=cpc) and your campaign is about a special promotion you have for organic juice (utm_campaign=organic_juice_promo).

To see this data in Analytics go to Reports > Acquisition > All Traffic > Source/Medium. Or if you want to compare the performance between campaigns just go to Reports > Acquisition > Campaigns > All Campaigns.

For Bing Ads, you can automate this process. Just make sure you enable Destination URL auto-tagging.

A few other tools you should consider:

Hotjar - an analytics tool that allows you to record visitors on your website, create heatmaps and more. It allows you to see first hand what the user is doing on the website, see if they have any struggles finding the info they need, and see how they scroll, click and spend their time.

Google Optimize - will help you test your website. You can send half of your users to see one variation of your page, and the other half a different one (also known as A/B testing) and see which one has a better performance and higher conversion rate.

Google Ads - don't forget that Ads has a very good Reports section that allows you to create custom reports and analyse data.

Google Data Studio - allows you to turn your data into nice-looking reports and dashboards that are easy to read, share and customize.

Yandex Metrica - a free alternative to both Google Analytics and Hotjar which allows you to analyze traffic, view heatmaps, and more.

The internet is full of different tools you can use for your analytics, but the ones above should be your first choice when you are just starting.

7.2 Conversion tracking

You cannot make data-driven decisions if you cannot associate a conversion (sale, lead, sign-up etc) with a specific channel or campaign. There are 3 main ways in Google Analytics that help you do this.

Goal tracking. If you have a confirmation page that the user lands on after he submits (also known as a "thank-you" page) you can set up a destination goal and track all the users that have gotten to it.

Event tracking. If you care about form submits, or any other type of button clicks that don't redirect to a thank-you page, you need to set up event tracking. It will allow you to track specific button clicks, video plays and more.

Ecommerce Tracking. If you are an ecommerce website, you might want to track all orders and have the order value shown to you. The implementation requires more code, but the results will be amazing. You'll be able to see analytics data in this format.

Product	Sales Performance				
	Product Revenue ↓	Unique Purchases	Quantity	Avg. Price	Avg. QTY
	$6,633.67 % of Total: 100.00% ($6,633.67)	78 % of Total: 100.00% (78)	92 % of Total: 100.00% (92)	$72.11 Avg for View: $72.11 (0.00%)	1.18 Avg for View: 1.18 (0.00%)
1. 5 Day Cleanse	$2,589.30 (39.03%)	13 (16.67%)	14 (15.22%)	$184.95	1.08
2. 3 Day Cleanse	$1,084.20 (16.34%)	8 (10.26%)	8 (8.70%)	$135.52	1.00
3. Special Offer 24 Bottles Kombucha	$1,054.60 (15.90%)	16 (20.51%)	20 (21.74%)	$52.73	1.25
4. Kombucha Raspberry	$294.57 (4.44%)	6 (7.69%)	9 (9.78%)	$32.73	1.50
5. 2 Day Cleanse	$238.00 (3.59%)	2 (2.56%)	2 (2.17%)	$119.00	1.00
6. Kombucha Passionfruit	$229.11 (3.45%)	4 (5.13%)	7 (7.61%)	$32.73	1.75
7. Sparkling Mango and Orange	$108.00 (1.63%)	3 (3.85%)	3 (3.26%)	$36.00	1.00
8. Sparkling Passionfruit	$108.00 (1.63%)	2 (2.56%)	3 (3.26%)	$36.00	1.50
9. Cola	$98.19 (1.48%)	3 (3.85%)	3 (3.26%)	$32.73	1.00
10. Lemon Lime and Bitters	$98.19 (1.48%)	3 (3.85%)	3 (3.26%)	$32.73	1.00

7.3 What metrics do you measure with PPC?

Once you have Google Analytics set up and your conversion tracking is working, it's time to see how your campaigns are performing. But what should you actually look at to understand if it works?

It's hard to have predetermined numbers which you need to see in your website engagement, as it's unique to your niche and type of content.

Analytics does a good job showing you some Benchmarking based on your type of business. You can see them in Reports > Audience > Benchmarking. It will look something like this.

Default Channel Grouping	Acquisition			Behavior			
	Sessions ↓	% New Sessions	New Users	Pages/Session	Avg. Session Duration	Bounce Rate	
	65.10% ▲ 1,043 vs. 1,405	1.65% ▲ 73.94% vs 71.97%	64.53% ▲ 1,099 vs 1,845	2.32% ▼ 2.65 vs 2.72	25.65% ▲ 00:01:47 vs 00:02:24	8.03% ▼ 57.96% vs 55.46%	
□ 1. Paid Search	-87.14% ▼ 1,346 vs 1,888	0.27% ▼	37.28% ▼ 866 vs 1363	11.48% ▲ 2.68 vs 2.31	33.87% ▲ 00:02:06 vs 00:01:28	7.26% ▲ 42.34% vs 47.52%	
□ 2. Organic Search	-74.38% ▼ 589 vs 6,126	2.15% ▲ 76.70% vs 74.40%	-75.84% ▼ 289 vs 3578	1.42% ▲	33.77% ▲ 00:01:35 vs 00:01:49	-14.74% ▼ 61.93% vs 55.67%	
□ 3. Social	-82.70% ▼ 187 vs 293	-0.07% ▼ 76.47% vs 73.04%	-82.71% ▼ 83 vs 629	5.57% ▼ 2.16 vs 2.27	35.86% ▼ 00:00:58 vs 00:01:29	-7.64% ▼ 69.49% vs 53.67%	
□ 4. Direct	-44.63% ▼ 966 vs 1,175	4.97% ▼	-43.87% ▼ 170 vs 2343	2.81% ▲	28.48% ▲	1.04% ▼ 73.52% vs 69.37%	
□ 5. Referral	-54.12% ▼ 36 vs 580	-28.23% ▼ 47.37% vs 45.98%	-93.66% ▼ 17 vs 91	-40.65% ▼ 1.99 vs 3.48	-36.79% ▼ 00:01:08 vs 00:02:04	18.60% ▲ 63.69% vs 59.39%	
□ 6. Display	-99.73% ▼ 4 vs 1,488	63.71% ▲ 75.00% vs 45.76%	-99.56% ▼ 3 vs 1,803	76.55% ▲ 7.25 vs 4.11	132.06% ▲ 00:04:06 vs 00:01:46	37.48% ▲ 100.00% vs 74.20%	
□ 7. (Other)	-100.00% ▼ 0 vs 620	-100.00% ▼ 0.00% vs 75.32%	-100.00% ▼ 0 vs 469	-100.00% ▼ 0.00 vs 2.32	-100.00% ▼ 00:00:00 vs 00:00:56	-100.00% ▼ 0.00% vs 69.68%	
□ 8. Email	-100.00% ▼ 0 vs 182	-100.00% ▼ 0.00% vs 60.44%	-100.00% ▼ 0 vs 110	-100.00% ▼ 0.00 vs 3.41	-100.00% ▼ 00:00:00 vs 00:01:50	-100.00% ▼ 0.00% vs 51.65%	
□ 9. Other Advertising	-100.00% ▼ 0 vs 6,739	-100.00% ▼ 0.00% vs 67.16%	-100.00% ▼ 0 vs 4,889	-100.00% ▼ 0.00 vs 1.42	-100.00% ▼ 00:00:00 vs 00:00:54	-100.00% ▼ 0.00% vs 75.14%	

The main metrics to look at would be: time on page (how long visitors stay on your website), bounce rate (the percentage of single-page sessions in which there was no interaction on the page) and pages/session (average time of pages viewed during a session).

Look at it from a common sense point of view. You want average session duration to be at least a minute and you want to have a very low bounce rate.

Compare the results between the channels. If your organic traffic has a higher engagement rate, check the search queries. Maybe it's because all organic traffic is coming from brand searches? Analyze the engagement between your pages. Maybe it's one page that brings the average down. See what can be fixed - or maybe that page is not highly targeted to your campaigns? A/B test and see if it makes a difference.

If your average time on page is 10 seconds, and your bounce rate is over 90%, something is not working well. Maybe it's not the page, but the traffic you send to it. Check your targeting within your campaign and analyze your search terms. Is the audience you're targeting right for your service? With a poorly set up campaign this happens often!

Conversion rates and transaction value

Great engagement is always a good sign. But is it directly correlated with your sales? Great engagement doesn't always mean good return on investment.

Analytics gives you data on how much you've spent and how much you've gotten back. If you're tracking events and goals you need to know how much each of them is worth to you...and do the math from there. If you have ecommerce tracking, Analytics will tell you how much money you've made.

A good conversion rate can be anywhere between 1% (for high value products) and 7-10% (for smaller sales, form submissions or calls).

Same as with engagement, check your conversion rate between campaigns and channels. Don't just look at the averages. See which campaigns give you the highest revenue, which landing pages perform better and keep testing if you see lower performance for some of them.

ROI, ROAS and Cost Data

When running any campaign, you will need to calculate your Return On Investment (ROI). Let's dive in with some real numbers.

If you want to calculate just your Return On Advertising Spending (ROAS) without overhead cost, the formula is: *ROAS = Total Revenue from Ads / Total Ad Cost*.

So, if you spent $1,000 on your campaigns in one month and generated a revenue of $5,000, then your return would be $5000 / $1000 = $5. That means that for every $1 spend on ads, you get $5!

Then, you probably want to calculate your ROI. The formula for ROI is *(Total Revenue From Ads – Total Cost)/ Total Cost*. Business overhead eats up a bit of your actual profits. If you spent $1,000 on your campaigns in one month and generated a revenue of $5,000 with a business overhead cost of $2,000, then your return would be (5000–(1000+2000) / (1000+2000))*100% = 2000/3000*100% = 66.67%. This means that for every $1 of total cost, you got $1.66 in profit.

Analytics already calculates ROAS for you. As you have Google Ads data automatically imported you can go to: Reports > Acquisition > Campaigns > Cost Analysis.

If you want to see other channel's cost data in Analytics, like Microsoft Ads or Facebook, you'll have to import your costs manually.

7.4 Attribution models

If you're using multiple channels to advertise, once you have conversion tracking setup, you want to make sure that you understand your user's journey before they become a lead or make an order. You can learn so much from it!

To do this, in Analytics, go to the left column, go to Conversions > Multi-Channel Funnels > Top Conversions Paths. As "Primary Dimension" choose "Source/Medium Path".

A tip: if one of your payment methods is PayPal, you'll be seeing that sales are coming from *paypal/referral*, and you might not know which channel to attribute it to. The report above is the only way to see which channel users used before they went to PayPal.

You can also see this data in Google Ads. It shows you results based on different attribution models (for Google Ads traffic only). Use this report to compare 2 different attribution models side-by-side. It's more advanced analytics, but I'm sure you can figure it out!

Once you're here, go to Attribution Modeling. There are a few ways you can look at your data:

- Last Click - gives all credit for the conversion to the last-clicked ad and corresponding keyword.
- First Click - gives all credit for the conversion to the first-clicked ad and corresponding keyword.
- Linear - distributes the credit for the conversion equally across all clicks on the path.
- Time Decay - gives more credit to clicks that happened closer in time to the conversion. Credit is distributed using a 7-day half-life.

- Position-based - gives 40% of credit to both the first-and last-clicked ads and corresponding keyword, with the remaining 20% spread out across the other clicks on the path.
- Data-driven - distributes credit for the conversion based on past data for this conversion action (this is only available to accounts with enough data.)

7.5 Testing for PPC

At this point, you should be able to set up a successful campaign and be able to analyze and optimize it to get the most out of it. Congrats! The purpose of this short section is to remind you to never stop testing. That's the only way to be successful

- Test your keywords to see which give you the most targeted user traffic
- Test your landing pages to see which are more relevant to the user's search
- Test your ads to see which message gets a higher CTR (click-through-rate) and a better Quality Score
- Test your messaging, wording, colors and offers.
  In addition, you should keep analyzing:
- Search terms used to get to your website
- Channels that bring you traffic
- User engagement based on the channels and campaigns
- Conversion rates and ROI to see how profitable your campaign is.

Chapter 8: Privacy & Advertising

I'm a huge fan of internet privacy.

Now, that seems a little disjointed coming from me, right? I have a blog. I post on social media. And for goodness sakes, I help run Discosloth, a search marketing company which literally functions by serving targeted ads to users.

But there's a big difference between the ability to do something, the need to do something, and actually doing something. I'll explain this now, and then a bit later I'll cover how I personally protect my privacy online.

All of the above is all well and good, you might say, but you own a company that sells ads. Sounds like I'm speaking out of my butt, right?

Here's the deal. I think that first, there is misinformation about just how much personal data is accessible by most advertisers, and second, this personal data is actually overvalued in general. Let's start with the first.

We run millions of dollars of ad campaigns each year, mostly on Google Ads. We're a Google Partner. We are good at targeting extremely granularly. If anyone could have access to personal data, it'd be us. But we don't. We can't really identify who we're targeting. We can narrow it down, and here's what we can find out:

1. **General location.** We can target fairly granularly - usually targeting radiuses around addresses (like 1 mile around 1600 Pennsylvania Ave) or zip codes (targeting only 72202) or general neighborhoods. But it is complicated for us to see that level of detail when we actually look in our Analytics and see who visited the site. We can't really get closer than zip code. We can see that 240 users from Colorado Springs visited the site, but that's about it.

2. **Demographics.** Google doesn't allow for very detailed demographic targeting, and some of the targeting is only available for certain types of ads, like the Display Network. Google can let us target a fairly broad demographic (say, females aged 35-44 in the top 10% of income) but they only have this sort of data for about half their audience (pretty much those who are signed into Gmail). Facebook Ads provides a much, much more detailed approach to personal targeting, and it's pretty creepy to be entirely honest. I don't like it.

3. **Retargeting.** This is actually a pretty useful advertising type, and the good thing is that I don't think it's too intrusive. If you've visited a website, we can serve ads to you for around 30 days afterwards (assuming you have cookies enabled in your browser). As a user you can block this, and in general I don't feel like it's too complicated or confusing for users.

And... that's about it. The power of Google Ads isn't that it targets users, though. The power of Google Ads is that it is intent-based. I can get to exactly the right person just by targeting search terms. No need for concern for ITP2, which is a new technology that Apple recently introduced to prevent intrusive cookies being placed.

8.1 Is highly targeted advertising even necessary?

But to the next thing - the necessity of targeted advertising in general. I really think the industry has fixated on the shiny new tech of hyper-targeting, and gets caught up in fantasies of buyer personas and custom intent and top-of-funnels and all sorts of ridiculous abbreviations.

A simple campaign targeting search terms and a general geo-location can get you 95% of the way to a perfect, profitable advertising strategy.

All the rest? Outsized effort for incremental gains. That last 5% is going to be the most expensive and most complicated 5% you'll ever work for, and for the vast majority of advertisers it simply is not worth it. Your advertising agency will spend 5X the time on that last 5% than they spent on your entire bottom 95%, and they'll be sure to charge you for it, too.

Here's the deal. Data is great and all, but if you get obsessed with data it makes you myopic. I've seen so many campaigns and agencies and managers develop a laser-beam approach to marketing. They're ridiculously focused on one specific approach, but oblivious to everything in the periphery.

Don't misread me: we're extremely data-driven as a company. Every facet of our campaigns is driven by data of some sort. The difference? We're targeting intent, not people.

We don't want to know someone's phone number, their mother's maiden name, their medical ailments, their favorite music, or what they ate for dinner. It's not that we ignore data. Again, it's just that we target intent, not people. Because intent is so much more powerful than demographics.

Focusing on demographics rather than intent means that you will lose every customer who falls outside your supposed target audience.

Just because the data says that a 27-year-old female with one child who lives in the 31205 zip code and has a household income of $50,000-75,000 is your perfect customer, it just doesn't mean that's true.

Google may want you to think it's true, because you'll spend a lot of money trying to acquire that perfect customer, but I wouldn't take that at face value.

Your ad agency may want you to think it's true, because their retainer can go sky high, but I wouldn't take that at face value either.

You probably just need a search campaign.

I believe that people deserve privacy. If they want it. And at whatever level they want it. Gil and I travel extensively - five or six countries a year. I work in coffeeshops or coworking spaces or airports most of the time, none of which are known to be super-secure environments. But more than that, I'm just a private person with private interests. I have a lot to hide. What sort of things do I have to hide?

- that I searched for the weather in Helsinki in June
- which banks I have accounts at

- that I like Buffy the Vampire Slayer
- what that strange 90's hand-drawn art style is called
- what sort of comedy I like

And the list goes on. None of my interests are harmful. I would just like to choose where to share them. If you want to know something about me, ask me.

Privacy is something that I personally pursue multiple methods of anonymization, cookie-deletion, and ad-blocking. How do I manage my internet privacy? Let's go through the list.

First, I use Firefox which I've found has been one of the most privacy-focused browsers for users along with Safari. The latest releases include ITP2 (intelligent tracking prevention) and make it extremely difficult for other entities (like Google) to track you without consent. Do you run Analytics on your site? You've probably noticed the increase in non-attributed "direct" visits. Where did these guys come from? Dunno. They're probably using Safari or Firefox

Second, I often use a VPN. And not just any old free proxy, but I chose a paid VPN based in a region with solid privacy laws and outside the jurisdiction of most superpowers.

Third, I have been trying to transition towards using DuckDuckGo instead of Google. I haven't been able to fully transition, because Google is still the best search engine in the world and it excels at almost every result. But, I want to give the underdog a try.

Fourth, I don't like social media. I'm still on it, mostly because of work, but it's not often used. Fifth, I run my own mail servers. In a world full of webmail, it's rare but I think it's very important to maintain control of your own email. It's the only fully distributed, personally maintainable, and totally ubiquitous communication service on the planet. Everyone has email. And it's super easy to control your own domain and mail servers.

I can talk out of my butt all day long, but it doesn't really matter if I don't do anything about it.

I believe in the importance of privacy. I also believe most people don't care. That's up to them. And as long as they don't care, companies are going to take advantage of that data and sell them as much as possible. I will happily continue running ads. If you don't like them, install an ad blocker! I already did.

Yet I also strongly believe that there's a better way to approach advertising. That's why I am intending to focus more and more on search engines like DuckDuckGo, which is exploding in popularity (I think they just passed one billion searches/mo which is pretty impressive if you ask me).

And yes, that's about a 0.98% market share. Tiny, right? That's how much people care about privacy. Under 1%. Hmm.

Chapter 9: Automation In PPC & What To Expect

You've probably heard it online: robots are coming to take our jobs!

Even as a digital marketer, you're probably not immune to the onslaught of articles talking about how artificial intelligence and machine learning are coming to take your job. I don't take such a drastic approach (stagecoach drivers also lost their jobs, but quickly changed over to taxi drivers!) but at the same time it's important to realize that your job will definitely change.

Based on a definition by Hubspot (and who would know better, if not them) marketing automation is the software and technologies that exist with the goal of, get this, automating marketing actions.

Many marketing departments have to automate repetitive tasks in order to perform at scale - like email, social media posts, website actions, etc. The technology of marketing automation makes these tasks easier.

But somewhere, the discussion about marketing automation evolved into more than just that. It's no longer just some email drip campaigns - it's fancy words and abbreviations like AI, ML, growth hacking, ClickFunnels, big data, Unbounce, Drift, and endless others.

In today's world users, albeit slowly, are appreciating honesty, transparency, and privacy more and more, we've suddenly become raw datasets in dozens of databases with all sorts of labels associated with our identities (and who doesn't like to be labeled?) We get dozens of emails when we sign up for a software trial. Then we keep getting the same email. Then we get emails from software "partners". Then we start getting phone calls, and seeing banner ads, and start dreaming about the software trial in our sleep.

They never seem to understand that…dude, I'm sorry, but I'm just not that into you if I ignored the first 20 emails.

Automation is everywhere, and not only is it getting more inconvenient for users, but it's getting harder for marketers. Sometimes it feels you simply have no choice, and there is so much noise around certain strategies that you think "this has to be good" even though based on your experience everyone you knows hates getting caught up in a click funnel or drip campaign.

How did we get swallowed up in this trend? How does it relate to pay-per-click advertising? And is anyone taking advantage of us by convincing us that automating things is good?

We're focused on Google Ads here, so we'll use it as a good example. Everyone who works in PPC knows how Google has slowly forced us to change our attitude about automation. It isn't all bad, of course, but we'll explore the pros and cons.

9.1 Pros of automation in Google Ads

When you listen to Google speaking about automation, all you'll hear is that automation helps. This has some nuggets of truth.

Automation helps most in these scenarios:

- You have a very small audience (either a super targeted local service or a product with limited amount of searches). Automation helps in finding all search term variations and helping maximize clicks.

- App Promotion campaigns work great with automated targeting as long as you have conversion tracking set up. Of course, there is no manual targeting option so there is little manual competition, which may be a reason.

- Shopping campaigns are also mostly automated, yet give great results. The only manual control you really have are adjustment of bids.

- If you have dozens of campaigns and no one is paying too much attention to them during management, automation means you can usually get by with fairly decent results.
- If you have no idea where to start and you need ideas and data before you build a manual campaign based off the automated data.

There are also some cons, however. Let's take a look at these and get a better idea of the landscape.

9.2 Cons of automation in Google Ads

While talking to a Google Ads representative, they told me that manual bidding may not even be an option soon. While I don't know if this is true or not, looking at some of the notifications of Google Ads makes me believe it.

This screenshot says that manual bids results in lower performance. But is this so?

Bidding   Back to previous bidding options

Manual CPC   ▾

☐ Help increase conversions with Enhanced CPC ⊙

⚠ Setting bids manually may result in **lower performance**. Use Smart Bidding to help improve results by using more signals to optimize your bids. Learn more

Let's check out Keyword Planner. Searching for "become a digital nomad" brings up all sorts of irrelevant searches that Google thinks are relevant. Likewise, if you just give Google Ads a list of keywords you know are relevant, you will absolutely appear for services that aren't relevant to your business. Unless, as in this example, your service has to do with becoming a digital nomad, finding specific jobs, giving some presentations, and a list of nomad millionaires on the same page.

	Search term	Match type	Added/Excluded	Ad group	Keyword
	Total: Filtered search ter...				
	become a digital nomad	Broad match	None	1. Awareness - Digital Nomads #2	being a nomad
	digital nomad indonesia	Broad match	None	1. Awareness - Digital Nomads #2	being a nomad
	digital nomad software engineer	Broad match	None	1. Awareness - Digital Nomads #2	being a nomad
	how to be a nomad artist	Broad match	None	1. Awareness - Digital Nomads #2	being a nomad
	how to be a nomad entrapeneur	Broad match	None	1. Awareness - Digital Nomads #2	being a nomad
	how to get visa as a digital nomad	Broad match	None	1. Awareness - Digital Nomads #2	being a nomad
	nomad millionaire	Broad match	None	1. Awareness - Digital Nomads #2	being a nomad
	nomadic life presentation	Broad match	None	1. Awareness - Digital Nomads #2	being a nomad
	things you need to live a nomad lifestyle	Broad match	None	1. Awareness - Digital Nomads #2	being a nomad

Automated bidding is also a huge problem. When choosing your bidding strategy, you can pick between manual and automated bidding. For manual, you determine the maximum price you're willing to pay for a click. Automated bidding decides it for you.

I tested a few campaigns to see if "maximize conversions" really brings better results than a purely manual bidding strategy.

And yes, it technically did improve the conversion rate by 61.5%. But looking at the CPC and the cost per conversion? The CPC increased by 79.1%. So who's the winner here? This technique automatically increased the minimum required bids for all other competitors, and the client is actually at a profit loss.

		Campaign	Avg. cost	Cost	Conversions	Cost / conv.	Conv. rate	Bid strategy type
☐	⚫	Home School - Search Maximize.com	$7.81	$952.53	16.00	$57.99	13.45%	Maximize conversions
☐	⚫	Home School - Search	$4.36	$693.59	13.00	$52.44	8.33%	Manual CPC

Auto applied ad suggestions is one of the worst offenders. I'm sorry, but this feature is just bad. Google is smart but is not creative. It doesn't know what is so special about your service, so when Google scrapes your site for words and attempts to generate an automatic ad, the results are almost universally terrible.

You'll also see Google suggesting a list of keywords that the system thinks is relevant for your business. We've seen so many clients just trust this and apply all suggestions. One of our clients, a luxury round-the-world flight service, started appearing for "student flights" and "vacation sites" - neither of which are remotely applicable.

The reality is that Google is learning and experimenting while taking your ad revenue. We get low quality traffic, low quality ads, and an increased cost per click as a results.

Another method we've noticed that increases the CPC even for low volume, noncommercial keywords is Google Grants. While it's fantastic that nonprofits can use Google Grants to advertise their programs, let's not get too excited.

Google Grants, for those not in the know, are accounts created for nonprofits. Google gives them the value of up to $10,000 a month to qualifying organizations. They can keep the grant as long as they follow stringent quality rules (no single-word keywords, no broad keywords, a high click through rate). Interesting that on all other accounts, Google recommends broad keywords.

These nonprofit accounts are limited to a $2 max cost per click. It's interesting that everyone on a Google Grants account is always maxed out at this rate in order to appear.

Essentially, Google Grants has created an artificial baseline, a $2 minimum CPC for everyone else who's actually paying for their traffic.

In short, the cons of automation is that it can significantly decrease your performance and increase your cost if you're not careful. It increases the average CPC for all businesses in your niche, which drives out small business.

And after all, Google doesn't have access to your financials. How do they know what your margin is? Something that seems profitable in an account is not necessarily profitable in real life.

Automation isn't bad. However, it is definitely changing the landscape. Ignoring it is an obvious error - just keep your eyes open and remember to assess everything with a critical slant. Don't blindly adopt any new technique without testing first.

In the end, as Google Ads experts, we should both embrace the inevitable and attempt to keep our distance from tactics that can lessen the effectiveness of our campaigns.

Because, after all, our entire purpose as account managers is to help our clients gain more sales through advertising: and at the lowest cost possible.

Afterword

Google Ads is one of the most powerful ways for a company to grow in the online world.

As social platforms continue to make it more difficult to see amazing results organically, without paying, running intent-focused ads on Google (and Microsoft Ads, as well) is a logical next step for companies that are either selling products or services and need to get in front of as many relevant people as possible.

The field will change, and most of the specific techniques found in this book won't even be relevant a few years down the road. However, the basic tenets will always be relevant: learning how to focus on users that have an intent for your product, learning how to structure a campaign in a logical manner, and learning how to write good copy that is simple, clear, and effective.

In the end, sometimes it is easy to get too close to your work. So keep this in mind: as a Google Ads expert -

whether you're a small business owner, a member of a corporate marketing team, or an agency - you're here to make advertising work as efficiently as possible. That's it! But it involves so much different aspects of work from conversion optimization, to customer communication, to research, to ad writing, that it's quite the complicated job at times.

Never stop learning, and always adapt to the changing field!

Resources For PPC Management

Helpful links & resources for further use

We've compiled a list of the most valuable resources for learning more about Google Ads. The Beginner's Guide To Google Ads is not meant as an exhaustive, end-all destination which transforms you into the world's best pay-per-click specialist. It's meant to give you a solid foundation and understanding of PPC strategies. There is more to be learned!

MARKETING TOOLS

Answer The Public
www.answerthepublic.com
Answer The Public is a great keyword exploration tool which helps find similar terms, phrases, and semantic possibilities for your keywords.

SERPsim

www.serpsim.com

Our favorite online tool for visualizing how meta descriptions and titles look in Google's search results.

SparkToro Trending

www.sparktoro.com/trending

Not as much a tool as an incredible way to keep up with marketing news, Trending analyzes which links the most popular marketers are sharing on Twitter, and lists them daily.

CoSchedule Headline Analyzer

www.coschedule.com/headline-analyzer

A great tool for analyzing your email subject lines, giving insight about which words to use, and the appropriate link for maximum open rates.

Nibbler Website Test

nibbler.silktide.com

A useful tool to analyze your website, giving you a rundown of things like speed, page content, broken links, and a huge range of other tips for optimization. It's not a perfect tool, and some of the suggestions need to be ignored, but it's a good way to get a quick handle on a website's health.

MARKETING BLOGS

SparkToro

www.sparktoro.com

Rand Fishkin, original writer of the Beginner's Guide To SEO and founder of Moz, next cofounded SparkToro as a tool to provide more info and data for the influencer marketing industry. He also blogs regularly. It's worth keeping up on his insights on SEO.

Moz Blog

www.moz.com/blog

One of the most valuable online resources for white-hat search engine optimization, with guest posts from a variety of well-respected marketers.

Kellogg Insight

https://insight.kellogg.northwestern.edu

For a high-level look at marketing theory, this is one of the best resources we've found. It's not very actionable or practical, to be honest, but that's to be expected from an academic site. It's still interesting and insightful, though.

MARKETING BOOKS

Blink - Malcolm Gladwell

Today's world is filled with a lot of data; sometimes, it can be too much data. Even though digital marketers have a massively valuable ability to sort through endless amounts of data, being too close to it can result in poor decisions, and that's exactly what this book is about. Expertise goes a long way in making decisions, and spreadsheets don't always tell the whole story. An excellent resource to help prevent yourself from becoming too myopic.

Lost and Founder - Rand Fishkin

We've read a lot of books by influential thinkers in the tech and marketing worlds. Many founders go either one of two ways when they're writing memoirs or reflections on their industry: they're either blatantly self-aggrandizing ("look at my sick Learjet!") or they're buried in technicalities and politics and unable to see the big picture. Either way, self-awareness is a rare quality. This book is very self-aware: sometimes painfully so. It's honest, transparent, and uncomfortable. It's worth it alone to hear an insider's opinion on the realities of venture capital vs bootstrapping.

Zero To One - Peter Thiel

A book developed from class notes from a course Peter Thiel, cofounder of PayPal, taught at Stanford, this short volume expounds on the simple concept of zero to one (creation) being more fundamentally productive than anything beyond that. It's a critical look at how simply creating things is a net benefit. I found it very insightful from a business perspective.

Trust Me, I'm Lying - Ryan Holiday

A guerrilla marketing expert and former American Apparel marketer, the often-controversial takes by Ryan Holiday are still extremely important. From a purely psychological basis, understanding how marketing and PR influences the public conversation can help you in everything from content creation to ad writing.

On Writing - Stephen King

That's right, it's not about marketing and it's not by a marketer. But this is one of the best books out there on clear communication, succinct writing, and how to get things done.

MARKETING GUIDES

The Beginner's Guide To PPC
www.discosloth.com/beginners-guide-to-ppc
Our very own guide, which we crafted with loving care and hope that everyone thinks it's as good as we do. It's our baby, but it's also been called "the sort of content I wish I'd created" and "if you need a resource for those learning PPC, this is the one." That obviously means you need to read it, too.

Beginner's Guide To SEO

www.moz.com/beginners-guide-to-seo

The original guide itself, rewritten over the years to keep up with the times, is still one of the most valuable resources out there. It was the inspiration behind our PPC guide, and I even had it printed out for reference when I was first diving into digital marketing.

Google Best Practices

support.google.com/adwords

Google's closest answer to a guide. This will provide helpful information if you're looking for specific insight into how to use Google Ads.

Academy For Ads

https://academy.exceedlms.com

Google's new home for certifications and study guides. It's worth going through their Fundamentals course and a few others, and getting certified.

100+ Google Ranking Factors

www.zyppy.com/seo-success-factors

An SEO-focused resource on ranking factors. A very useful and very informed guide— it's worth learning about this, regardless of your specific niche!

Printed in Great Britain
by Amazon